POULTRY FEED FORMULA

Easiest Way To Make Your Own Poultry Feed.

Handbook for poultry feed formulations

Patrick Odega

COPYRIGHT PAGE

TABLE OF CONTENTS

INTRODUCTION

This formula will serve as a guide for you when you create your own chicken feed. It is a sure path to genuine liberated independence and advancement. The essence of this book or formula is to guide you to mix feed stuff yourself and also save you over 45% cost of production and you are sure of the balanced ratio.

Formulating feed yourself gives you the liberation from excessive feed cost, inconsistent supply, and less quality feeds. The feedstuff used here is already available in our local markets.

Therefore, I implore you to mix your poultry feeds yourself or take any feed formats of your choice to the feed mill and insist they followed the recommended formula. Because only this method can give you full satisfaction and relieve you from unnecessary worry about the quality of the feeds and how it's being compounded.

You now have full control of your feed and the desires that result in your poultry birds. This formula has been tested many times and the result it brings is excellent and far better than many feeds mill factory produces on a daily basis.

TYPES OF CHICKEN FEED

The correct type of feed for your chickens depends on two things: their age and whether they are meat birds or laying birds.

Chick starter: Exactly what it sounds like, chick starter is for the first (usually six) weeks of your baby chicks' lives. This is typically 22 to 24 percent protein for meat birds (called broiler starter) and 20 percent protein for laying breeds. You can buy medicated or unmedicated chick starter. Most people use a medicated feed, but organic and pastured small farms often use unmedicated feed.

Grower pullet: After chick starter, young pullets that are destined for a laying flock are put on a lower-protein diet to slow growth to allow strong bones and adult body weight before laying begins. If the protein is too high, development happens quickly and the birds lay too early. Grower pullet rations typically have 18 percent protein and are fed until the chicks are 14 weeks of age.

Pullet developer or finisher: At 14 weeks, young pullets can be lowered to a 16 percent protein feed until they begin laying. Some feed lines don't distinguish between this stage and the grower stage and just have a grower-finisher that is somewhere in the middle protein-wise.

Layer rations: Laying hens at maturity (around 22 weeks of age) require a 16 to 18 percent protein level and extra calcium and minerals for strong eggshells. Don't feed layer rations to birds younger than this age as it damages their kidneys due to the high amounts of calcium and phosphorus. However, roosters can eat laying rations.

Broiler rations: These high-protein feeds are for meat birds, particularly Cornish X Rock crosses that grow extremely fast. Broiler rations are typically 18 to 20 percent protein. This is sometimes called "grower-finisher" feed. For heritage and pastured meat birds, protein content can be lowered to 16 percent after 12 weeks of age until butchering.

Some may choose to keep the heritage meat birds on the higher grower-finisher rations until slaughter.

If you want to reduce the amount of feed you need for your chickens, raise them on pasture. They'll be able to find enough insects, bugs, weeds, grasses, and seeds to stay healthy. They'll still need some supplemental feed, though.

WHAT IS FEED FORMULATION?

The process of determining the amounts of feed
ingredients that must be mixed to make a single uniform
diet for animals to meet all of their nutrient requirements
is known as feed formulation.

Forms of feed

Chicken and poultry feed comes in three forms: crumbles,
pellets, and mash. Crumbles are excellent if you can get
them, but pellets are sometimes the only form available.

Mash is usually used for baby chicks, but it can be mixed
with warm water to make a thick oatmeal-like treat for
chickens. However, it must be fed right away or else it
spoils and becomes moldy, so don't let mixed mash sit
around.

METHOD OF PROCESSING CERTAIN FEEDSTUFFS

BLOOD MEAL: Collected blood meal should be boiled till coagulation takes place. Sun dried the coagulated blood and grind, this becomes blood meal

BONE MEAL: Collected animal bones are burnt till it turns whitish. At this point it becomes brittle. Pound and grind the brittle to become **bone meal**

SOYABEAN MEAL: Roast or fry the soya bean in a frying pan like groundnut till it turns brownish. Grind to have your soya bean meal.

Frying the soya bean becomes necessary because soya bean contains an anti nutritional element which is dangerous to every living thing. This is destroyed in the course of roasting/frying

FISH MEAL: Sun-dried the fish, crayfish, or their waste/crumbs, pound and grind to have your fish meal

GROUNDNUT CAKE: Fry and grind the groundnut seed, thoroughly extract the oil from the bulky lump, Cut the lump into pieces and fry. Pound and grind for animal feed.

GRAINS: (maize, guinea corn, millet etc) are ground to enhance homogeneity and digestibility.

HOW TO MIX FEED

Step by step instruction on how to mix your own poultry feed.

Take your recipe from the poultry feed formula. (That is choose the format of your choice from poultry formula.

Gather all the ingredients needed for the feed

Select all the needed tools:

- ✓ 1 large scale (spring balance) that can measure 50kg
- ✓ Bucket
- ✓ Shovel
- ✓ Clean floor or thick plastic sheet.

Mix all the "small amount ingredients" (according to your recipe) with 5 to 10kg maize (bran) thoroughly in a bucket or on the floor. You can use your hands or a small shovel.

Note: Make sure the maize (bran) is completely dry (no moisture) so the ingredients do not clumb

Add the mixture with the "small amount ingredients" on top of a larger amount of maize (bran) like 50kg or 100kg.Use a shovel to mix it thoroughly. Take your time to do this till you have a uniform mixture.

Now you can add all the other large amount ingredients (according to your recipe) on the floor and mix everything thoroughly with a shovel till a uniform mix is achieved.

Take your time to do this properly. Now your feed is ready to use!

You can store the feed in bags in a dry place, lifted from the floor or you can keep it on a pile. Make sure you stir the whole pile every day to maintain the quality
of the feed.

General tips:
- Use the precise measurement when the micro - ingredients.
- Use clean tools and equipment.
- When you have questions don't hesitate to ask!

CHAPTER ONE
Chick Mash Feed

Characteristics Of Chick Mash Feed

This is the feed fed day old pullets between the ages of 0-8 weeks: therefore, chick's mash should

1.   Contain 19-22% crude protein
2.   5-7.5% crude fibre
3.   Energy level: 2,600-2,650kcal/kg
4.   Fats content: 1.0%
5.   Methionine: 0.8%
6.   Lysine: 1.0%
7.   Calcium: 1 -1.2%
8.   Phosophorus: 0.40 – 0.7%
9.   Common salt: 0.30 – 0.35%

10.   Vitamin Premix 0.25 – 0.35%

20% CRUDE PROTEIN CHICKS MASH

INGREDIENT	IN 100KG	IN 500KG	IN 1000KG
Maize	45.00	225.00	450.00
Brewer spent grain	14.00	70.00	140.00
Cotton seed meal	32.40	162.00	324.00
Blood meal	5.00	25.00	50.00
Oyster/periwinkle shell	3.00	15.00	30.00
Salt	0.30	1.50	3.00
Vitamin Premix	0.30	1.50	3.00

22% CRUDE PROTEIN CHICKS MASH

INGREDIENT	IN 100KG	IN 500KG	IN 1000KG
Maize	36.00	180.00	360.00
Beniseed	2.00	10.00	20.00
Maize bran	18.00	90.00	180.00
Palm kernel cake	14.00	70.00	140.00
Groundnut cake	20.00	100.00	200.00
Bone meal	3.00	15.00	30.00
Salt	0.30	1.50	3.00
Lysine	0.20	1.00	2.00
Methionine	0.20	1.00	2.00
Vitamin Premix	0.30	1.50	3.00
Blood meal	6.00	30.00	50.00

21% CRUDE PROTEIN CHICKS MASH

INGREDIENT	IN 100KG	IN 500KG	IN 1000KG
Guinea corn	42.00	210.00	420.00
Wheat bran	30.00	150.00	300.00
Cotton seed meal	10.00	50.00	100.00
Fish meal	14.00	71.00	142.00
Bone meal	3.00	15.00	30.00
Salt	0.30	1.50	3.00
Lysine	0.10	0.50	1.00
Methionine	0.10	0.50	1.00
Vitamin Premix	0.30	1.50	3.00

22% CRUDE PROTEIN CHICKS MASH

INGREDIENT	IN 100KG	IN 500KG	IN 1000KG
Guinea corn	58.00	290.00	580.00
Wheat bran	14.00	70.00	140.00
Cotton seed meal	14.00	70.00	140.00
Fish meal	6.50	33.00	66.00
Blood meal	3.30	16.50	33.00
Limestone	3.20	16.00	32.00
Lysine	1.15	0.75	1.50
Methionine	0.20	1.00	2.00
Salt	0.30	1.50	3.00
Vitamin Premix	0.25	1.25	2.50

CHAPTER TWO
Layers Mash

Characteristics Of Layers Mash (Pol)

This feed is fed from 18-20 weeks to point of lay (POL) to the time they had finished laying (spent layers) and are due for culling.
This feed should:

1.   Contain 16 – 18% crude protein

2.   Energy level: 2,500 – 2,700 kcal/kg
3.   Fibre level: 15 – 25 %
4.   Calcium: 3.00 – 3.5 %
5.   Phosphorus: 0.35 – 0.6 %
6.   Methionine: 0.6%
7.   Lysine: 0.6 – 0.7 %
8.   Common salt: 0.35 – 0.5 %
9.   Vitamin premix 0.35 – 0.5%

18% CRUDE PROTEIN LAYERS MASH

INGREDIENT	IN 100KG	IN 500KG	IN 1000KG
Guinea corn	46.50	232.00	465.00
Maize bran	23.00	115.00	230.00
Groundnut cake	14.00	70.00	140.00
Blood meal	5.00	25.00	50.00
Limestone	7.50	37.50	75.00
Bone meal	3.15	15.75	31.5
Salt	0.35	1.75	3.50
Vitamin Premix	0.50	2.50	5.00

18% CRUDE PROTEIN LAYERS MASH

INGREDIENT	IN 100KG	IN 500KG	IN 1000KG
Maize	48.00	240.00	480.00
Rice offal	16.00	80.00	160.00
Soya bean meal	18.65	93.25	185.50
Blood meal	6.00	30.00	60.00
Limestone	7.50	37.50	75.00
Bone meal	3.00	15.00	30.00
Salt	0.35	1.75	3.50
Vitamin Premix	0.50	2.50	5.00

18% CRUDE PROTEIN LAYERS MASH

INGREDIENT	IN 100KG	IN 500KG	IN 1000KG
Millet	6.00	30.00	60.00
Guinea corn	37.00	185.00	370.00
Rice bran	18.00	90.00	180.00
Fish meal	10.30	51.50	103.00
Cotton seed meal	18.00	90.00	180.00
Limestone	7.00	35.00	70.00
Bone meal	3.00	15.00	30.00
Salt	0.35	1.75	3.50
Vitamin Premix	0.35	1.75	3.50

18.5% CRUDE PROTEIN LAYERS MASH

INGREDIENT	IN 100KG	IN 500KG	IN 1000KG
Cassava meal	3.00	15.00	30.00
Guinea corn	46.00	230.00	460.00
Rice offal	13.50	67.50	135.00
Groundnut cake	23.55	117.75	235.50
Blood meal	2.50	12.50	25.00
Lysine	0.15	0.75	1.50
Methionine	0.10	0.5	1.00
Salt	0.35	1.75	3.50
Limestone	7.50	37.50	75.00
Oyster/Periwinkle shell	3.00	15.00	30.00
Vitamin Premix	0.35	1.75	3.50

18 % CRUDE PROTEIN LAYERS MASH

INGREDIENTS	IN 100KG	IN 500KG	1N 1000KG
Maize	49.00	245.00	490.00
Wheat bran	25.00	125.00	250.00
Fish meal	13.00	65.00	130.00
Blood meal	2.00	10.00	20.00
Limestone	7.00	35.00	70.00
Bone meal	3.00	15.00	30.00
Salt	0.35	1.75	3.50
Vitamin premix	0.40	2.00	4.00
Lysine	0.10	0.50	1.00
Methionine	0.15	0.75	1.50

CHAPTER THREE

Broilers Starter Mash

Characteristics Of Broiler Starter Mash Feed

This feed is fed from day old to 4-5 weeks of age. This feed should:

1. Contain 22 - 24 % crude protein
2. Energy level: 3000 and above
3. Low fibre level
4. Calcium 0.6 – 0.8 %
5. Phosphorus: 0.4 – 0.6 %

6. Vitamin premix: 0.25-0.35
7. The energy content can be boosted with oil if
   necessary

22 % CRUDE PROTEIN BROILER STARTER MASH FEED

INGREDIENTS	IN 100KG	IN 500KG	1N 1000KG
Maize	63.00	315.00	630.00
Rice offal	10.00	50.00	100.00
Fish meal	25.00	128.25	256.50
Limestone	0.50	2.50	5.00
Salt	0.35	1.75	3.50
Vitamin premix	0.50	2.50	5.00

22 % CRUDE PROTEIN BROILERS STARTER MASH

INGREDIENTS	IN 100KG	IN 500KG	1N 1000KG
Guinea corn	53.50	267.50	535.00
Beniseed	6.15	40.75	81.50
Soya bean meal	30.50	152.50	305.00
Palm kernel cake	4.00	20.00	40.00
Bone meal	3.00	15.00	30.00
Salt	0.50	2.50	5.00
Vitamin premix	0.35	1.75	3.50

22 % CRUDE PROTEIN BROILERS STARTER MASH

INGREDIENTS	IN 100KG	IN 500KG	1N 1000KG
Maize	16.00	80.00	160.00
Guinea corn	45.00	225.00	450.00
Groundnut cake	35.00	175.00	350.00
Palm oil	0.30	1.50	3.00
Bone meal	3.00	15.00	30.00
Salt	0.35	1.75	3.50
Vitamin premix	0.35	1.75	3.50

22 % CRUDE PROTEIN BROILERS STARTER MASH

INGREDIENTS	IN 100KG	IN 500KG	1N 1000KG
Maize	61.50	307.50	615.00
Groundnut cake	30.15	150.75	301.50
Blood meal	4.00	20.00	40.00
Bone meal	3.00	15.00	30.00
Salt	0.35	1.75	3.50
Vitamin premix	0.50	2.50	5.00
Palm oil	0.50	2.50	5.00

23 % CRUDE PROTEIN BROILERS STARTER MASH

INGREDIENTS	IN 100KG	IN 500KG	1N 1000KG
Maize	56.00	280.00	560.00
Groundnut cake	40.30	201.50	403.00
Bone meal	3.00	15.00	30.00
Salt	0.35	1.75	3.50
Vitamin premix	0.35	1.75	3.50

23 % CRUDE PROTEIN BROILERS STARTER MASH

INGREDIENTS	IN 100KG	IN 500KG	1N 1000KG
Maize	53.50	267.50	535.00
Beniseed	5.50	27.50	55.00
Groundnut cake	37.65	188.25	376.50
Salt	0.35	1.75	3.50
Bone meal	2.65	13.25	26.50
Vitamin premix	0.35	1.75	3.50

23 % CRUDE PROTEIN BROILERS STARTER MASH

INGREDIENTS	IN 100KG	IN 500KG	1N 1000KG
Maize	55.00	275.00	550.00
Soya bean meal	41.35	206.75	413.50
Bone meal	3.00	15.00	30.00
Salt	0.30	1.50	3.00
Vitamin premix	0.35	1.75	3.50

23 % CRUDE PROTEIN BROILERS STARTER MASH

INGREDIENTS	IN 100KG	IN 500KG	1N 1000KG
Maize	70.00	350.00	700.00
Fish meal	26.35	131.75	263.50
Bone meal	3.00	15.00	30.00
Salt	0.30	1.50	3.00
Vitamin premix	0.35	1.75	3.50

23 % CRUDE PROTEIN BROILERS STARTER MASH

INGREDIENTS	IN 100KG	IN 500KG	1N 1000KG
Guinea corn	59.00	295.00	590.00
Beniseed	4.00	20.00	40.00
Bone meal	3.00	15.00	30.00
Soya bean meal	30.30	151.50	303.00
Salt	0.35	1.75	3.50
Vitamin premix	0.35	1.75	3.50
Blood meal	3.00	15.00	30.00

23 % CRUDE PROTEIN BROILERS STARTER MASH

INGREDIENTS	IN 100KG	IN 500KG	1N 1000KG
Maize	64.00	320.00	640.00
Beniseed	2.00	10.00	20.00
Palm kernel cake	6.00	30.00	60.00
Bone meal	3.00	15.00	30.00
Salt	0.35	1.75	3.50
Blood meal	2.00	10.00	20.00
Vitamin premix	0.35	1.75	3.50
Fish meal	22.30	111.50	223.00

24 % CRUDE PROTEIN BROILERS STARTER MASH

INGREDIENTS	IN 100KG	IN 500KG	1N 1000KG
Guinea corn	71.00	355.00	710.00
Fish meal	25.35	126.75	253.50
Bone meal	3.00	15.00	30.00
Salt	0.30	1.50	3.00
Vitamin premix	0.35	1.75	3.50

24 % CRUDE PROTEIN BROILERS STARTER MASH

INGREDIENTS	IN 100KG	IN 500KG	1N 1000KG
Millet	18.00	90.00	180.00
Maize	51.80	259.00	518.00
Fish meal	27.00	135.00	270.00
Bone meal	2.50	12.50	25.00
Salt	0.35	1.75	3.50
Vitamin premix	0.35	1.75	3.50

24 % CRUDE PROTEIN BROILERS STARTER MASH

INGREDIENTS	IN 100KG	IN 500KG	1N 1000KG
Guinea corn	54.50	272.50	545.00
Soya bean meal	41.80	209.00	418.00
Bone meal	2.50	12.50	25.00
Vitamin premix	0.35	1.75	3.50
Salt	0.35	1.75	3.50
Palm oil	0.50	2.50	5.00

24 % CRUDE PROTEIN BROILERS STARTER MASH

INGREDIENTS	IN 100KG	IN 500KG	1N 1000KG
Maize	56.70	283.50	567.00
Wheat bran	1.00	5.00	10.00
Groundnut cake	32.90	164.50	329.00
Blood meal	5.35	26.75	53.50
Bone meal	3.00	15.00	30.00
Salt	0.30	1.50	3.00
Vitamin premix	0.25	1.25	2.50
Palm oil	0.50	2.50	5.00

24 % CRUDE PROTEIN BROILERS STARTER MASH

INGREDIENTS	IN 100KG	IN 500KG	1N 1000KG
Maize	47.25	236.25	472.50
Guinea corn	22.50	112.50	225.00
Fish meal	24.40	122.00	244.00
Blood meal	2.15	10.75	21.50
Bone meal	3.00	15.00	30.00
Salt	0.35	1.75	3.50
Vitamin premix	0.35	1.75	3.50

CHAPTER FOUR
Broilers Finisher

Characteristic Of Broiler Finisher Mash

This is fed the age of 4-5 weeks to 9-10 weeks old .This feed should

1 .Contain: 20-22 % crude protein
2. Energy level: 2800 – 3000 kcal/kg
3. Fibre level higher than broiler starter about 7.5%
4. Calcium: 0.6 – 0.8 %
5. Phosphorus: 0.4 – 0.8 %
6. Vitamin premix: 0.25 – 0.5 %

20% CRUDE PROTEIN BROILERS FINISHER MASH

INGREDIENTS	IN 100KG	IN 500KG	1N 1000KG
Maize	64.00	320.00	640.00
Groundnut cake	32.30	161.50	323.00
Bone meal	3.00	15.00	30.00
Salt	0.35	1.75	3.50
Vitamin premix	0.35	1.75	3.50

20 % CRUDE PROTEIN BROILERS FINISHER MASH

INGREDIENTS	IN 100KG	IN 500KG	1N 1000KG
Guinea corn	60.00	300.00	600.00
Rice offal	10.00	50.00	100.00
Soya bean meal	22.65	113.25	226.50
Bone meal	3.00	15.00	30.00
Blood meal	3.70	18.50	37.00
Salt	0.35	1.75	3.50
Vitamin premix	0.30	1.50	3.00

20 % CRUDE PROTEIN BROILERS FINISHER MASH

INGREDIENTS	IN 100KG	IN 500KG	1N 1000KG
Guinea corn	70.00	350.00	700.00
Fish meal	17.45	87.25	174.50
Limestone	4.00	20.00	40.00
Salt	0.30	1.50	3.00
Vitamin premix	0.25	1.25	2.50
Palm kernel cake	8.00	40.00	80.00

20 % CRUDE PROTEIN BROILERS FINISHER MASH

INGREDIENTS	IN 100KG	IN 500KG	1N 1000KG
Guinea	63.00	315.00	630.00
Groundnut	28.45	142.25	284.50
Rice bran	5.00	25.00	50.00
Bone meal	3.00	15.00	30.00
Salt	0.30	1.50	3.00
Vitamin premix	0.25	1.25	2.50

20 % CRUDE PROTEIN BROILERS FINISHER MASH

INGREDIENTS	IN 100KG	IN 500KG	1N 1000KG
Maize	42.00	210.00	420.00
Guinea corn	21.00	105.00	210.00
Groundnut cake	18.45	92.25	184.50
Soya bean meal	8.00	40.00	80.00
Wheat bran	5.00	25.00	50.00
Bone meal	3.00	15.00	30.00
Salt	0.30	1.50	3.00
Vitamin premix	0.25	1.25	2.50
Blood meal	2.00	10.00	20.00

21 % CRUDE PROTEIN BROILERS FINISHER MASH

INGREDIENTS	IN 100KG	IN 500KG	1N 1000KG
Maize	38.00	190.00	380.00
Cassava meal	9.00	45.00	90.00
Palm kernel	16.40	82.00	164.00
Groundnut cake	33.00	165.00	330.00
Bone meal	3.00	15.00	30.00
Salt	0.30	1.50	3.00
Vitamin premix	0.30	1.50	3.00

21 % CRUDE PROTEIN BROILERS FINISHER MASH

INGREDIENTS	IN 100KG	IN 500KG	1N 1000KG
Millet	12.00	60.00	120.00
Maize	49.45	247.25	494.50
Cottonseed meal	12.00	60.00	120.00
Soya bean meal	19.00	95.00	190.00
Blood meal	4.00	20.00	40.00
Bone meal	3.00	15.00	30.00
Salt	0.30	1.50	3.00
Vitamin premix	0.25	1.25	2.50

21 % CRUDE PROTEIN BROILERS FINISHER MASH

INGREDIENTS	IN 100KG	IN 500KG	1N 1000KG
Maize	60.40	302.00	640.00
Wheat bran	15.00	75.00	150.00
Fish meal	21.00	105.00	210.00
Salt	0.30	1.50	3.00
Bone meal	3.00	15.00	30.00
Vitamin premix	0.30	1.50	3.00

21 % CRUDE PROTEIN BROILERS FINISHER MASH

INGREDIENTS	IN 100KG	IN 500KG	1N 1000KG
Maize	40.00	200.00	400.00
Guinea corn	20.00	100.00	200.00
Rice bran	5.00	25.00	50.00
Groundnut cake	15.45	77.25	154.50
Soya bean meal	13.00	65.00	130.00
Blood meal	3.00	15.00	30.00
Salt	0.30	1.50	3.00
Bone meal	3.00	15.00	30.00
Vitamin premix	0.20	1.25	2.50

22 % CRUDE PROTEIN BROILERS FINISHER MASH

INGREDIENTS	IN 100KG	IN 500KG	1N 1000KG
Maize	53.40	267.00	534.00
Rice bran	6.50	32.50	65.00
Groundnut cake	36.60	183.00	366.00
Bone meal	3.00	15.00	30.00
Salt	0.30	1.50	3.00
Vitamin premix	0.20	1.00	2.00

22 % CRUDE PROTEIN BROILERS FINISHER MASH

INGREDIENTS	IN 100KG	IN 500KG	1N 1000KG
Guinea corn	61.50	307.50	515.00
Maize bran	10.00	50.00	100.00
Sunflower meal	8.20	41.00	82.00
Fish meal	16.75	83.76	167.50
Bone meal	3.00	15.00	30.00
Salt	0.30	1.50	3.00
Vitamin premix	0.25	1.25	2.50

22 % CRUDE PROTEIN BROILERS FINISHER MASH

INGREDIENTS	IN 100KG	IN 500KG	1N 1000KG
Guinea corn	20.00	100.00	200.00
Maize	39.00	195.00	390.00
Groundnut cake	21.40	107.00	214.00
Palm kernel cake	10.70	53.50	107.00
Blood meal	5.35	26.75	53.50
Bone meal	3.00	15.00	30.00
Salt	0.30	1.50	3.00
Vitamin premix	0.25	1.25	2.50

21.5 % CRUDE PROTEIN BROILERS FINISHER MASH

INGREDIENTS	IN 100KG	IN 500KG	1N 1000KG
Maize	43.40	217.00	434.00
Guinea corn	16.75	83.75	167.50
Groundnut cake	21.30	106.50	213.00
Soya bean meal	15.00	75.00	150.00
Bone meal	3.00	15.00	30.00
Salt	0.30	1.50	3.00
Vitamin premix	0.25	1.25	2.50

21.5 % CRUDE PROTEIN BROILERS FINISHER MASH

INGREDIENTS	IN 100KG	IN 500KG	1N 1000KG
Millet	13.30	66.50	133.00
Guinea corn	26.44	132.20	264.40
Cotton seed meal	22.60	113.00	226.00
Palm kernel meal	22.56	112.80	225.60
Fish meal	11.50	57.50	115.00
Oyster/periwinkle shell	3.00	15.00	30.00
Salt	0.30	1.50	3.00
Vitamin premix	0.25	1.25	2.50
Methionine	0.5	0.25	0.5

CHAPTER FIVE
Grower Mash

Characteristics Of Growers Mash

This is fed to pullets from 9-20 weeks or to the point of lay (POL).Growers mash should contain:

1. 15 – 18% crude protein.
2. Energy level : 2500 – 2700 kcal/kg.
3. Fibre level : 7.5 -10 %
4. Fats : 0.5 % - 1.0 %
5. Methionine : 0.6 – 0.7%
6. Lysine : : 0.6 – 0.7%
7. Calcium : 1 – 0.10 %
8. Phosphorus : 0.3 – 0.4 %
9. Common salt : 0.30 – 0.35
10. Vitamin premix : 0.30 – 0.5 %

16 % CRUDE PROTEIN GROWERS MASH

INGREDIENTS	IN 100KG	IN 500KG	1N 1000KG
Maize	45.35	226.75	453.50
Rice offal	35.00	175.00	350.00
Fish meal	13.20	66.00	132.00
Blood meal	2.85	14.25	28.50
Bone meal	3.00	15.00	30.00
Salt	0.30	1.50	3.00
Vitamin premix	0.30	1.50	3.00

17 % CRUDE PROTEIN GROWERS MASH

INGREDIENTS	IN 100KG	IN 500KG	1N 1000KG
Guinea corn	56.00	280.00	560.00
Wheat offal	28.00	140.00	280.00
Groundnut cake	11.40	57.00	114.00
Blood meal	2.00	10.00	20.00
Salt	0.30	1.50	3.00
Vitamin premix	0.30	1.50	3.00
Bone meal	2.00	10.00	20.00

18 % CRUDE PROTEIN GROWERS MASH

INGREDIENTS	IN 100KG	IN 500KG	1N 1000KG
Maize	44.00	220.00	440.00
Rice bran	29.00	145.00	290.00
Groundnut cake	23.30	116.50	233.00
Limestone	3.00	15.00	30.00
Salt	0.35	1.75	3.50
Vitamin premix	0.35	1.75	3.50

18 % CRUDE PROTEIN GROWERS MASH

INGREDIENTS	IN 100KG	IN 500KG	1N 1000KG
Guinea corn	33.00	165.00	330.00
Palm kernel cake	58.30	291.50	583.00
Blood meal	5.00	25.00	50.00
Bone meal	3.00	15.00	30.00
Salt	0.35	1.75	3.50
Vitamin premix	0.35	1.75	3.50

18 .5% CRUDE PROTEIN GROWERS MASH

INGREDIENTS	IN 100KG	IN 500KG	1N 1000KG
Guinea corn	51.00	255.00	510.00
Maize bran	25.00	125.00	250.00
Soya bean meal	17.95	89.75	179.50
Blood meal	2.00	10.00	20.00
Bone meal	3.00	15.00	30.00
Salt	0.30	1.75	3.50
Lysine	0.20	1.00	2.00
Methionine	0.20	1.00	2.00
Vitamin premix	0.30	1.50	3.00

18 % CRUDE PROTEIN GROWERS MASH

INGREDIENTS	IN 100KG	IN 500KG	1N 1000KG
Wheat meal	51.00	255.00	510.00
Rice offal	25.00	125.00	250.00
Groundnut cake	18.35	91.75	183.50
Blood meal	2.00	10.00	20.00
Oyster/periwinkle shell	3.00	15.00	30.00
Salt	0.35	1.75	3.50
Vitamin premix	0.30	1.50	3.00

CHAPTER SIX

Turkey Starter Feed

28% CRUDE PROTEIN TURKEY STARTER MASH (0-8 WEEKS)

INGREDIENTS	IN 100KG	IN 500KG	1N 1000KG
Maize	30.00	150.00	300.00
Guinea corn	15.50	77.50	155.00
Rice bran	3.00	15.00	30.00
Blood meal	5.75	28.75	57.50
Groundnut cake	42.00	210.00	420.00
Bone meal	3.00	15.00	30.00
Salt	0.30	1.50	3.00
Vitamin premix	0.45	2.25	4.50

28.5% CP PROTEIN TURKEY STARTER MASH

INGREDIENTS	IN 100KG	IN 500KG	1N 1000KG
Maize	26.55	132.75	265.50
Soya bean meal	52.70	263.50	527.00
Palm kernel meal	17.00	85.00	170.00
Bone meal	3.00	15.00	30.00
Salt	0.35	1.75	3.50
Vitamin premix	0.40	2.00	4.00

CHAPTER SEVEN
Turkey Finisher Mash

21.5% CP PROTEIN TURKEY FINISHER MASH

INGREDIENTS	IN 100KG	IN 500KG	1N 1000KG
Guinea corn	77.00	385.00	770.00
Fish meal	15.45	77.25	154.50
Blood meal	3.80	19.00	38.00
Bone meal	3.00	15.00	30.00
Salt	0.35	1.75	3.50
Vitamin premix	0.40	2.00	4.00

23% CP PROTEIN TURKEY FINISHER MASH

INGREDIENTS	IN 100KG	IN 500KG	1N 1000KG
Maize	56.00	280.00	560.00
Groundnut cake	26.10	130.50	261.00
Wheat bran	7.00	35.00	70.00
Blood meal	6.50	32.50	65.00
Limestone	3.50	17.50	35.00
Salt	0.40	2.00	4.00
Vitamin premix	0.50	2.50	5.00

CHAPTER FIFTEEN
Duck Layer Mash

21% CP PROTEIN TURKEY GROWER MASH

(9-20WEEKS)

INGREDIENTS	IN 100KG	IN 500KG	1N 1000KG
Guinea corn	51.70	258.50	517.00
Beniseed	4.00	20.00	40.00
Soyabean meal	27.10	135.50	271.00
Palm kernel meal	13.50	67.50	135.00
Bone meal	3.00	15.00	30.00
Salt	0.30	1.50	3.00
Vitamin premix	0.40	2.00	4.00

22.5% CP PROTEIN TURKEY GROWER MASH

INGREDIENTS	IN 100KG	IN 500KG	1N 1000KG
Millet	18.45	92.25	184.50
Maize	37.00	185.00	370.00
Rice bran	12.00	60.00	120.00
Groundnut cake	16.50	82.50	165.00
Fish meal	7.90	39.50	79.00
Blood meal	4.00	20.00	40.00
Limestone	3.50	17.50	35.00
Salt	0.30	1.50	3.00
Vitamin premix	0.35	1.75	3.50

CHAPTER NINE
Turkey Layer Mash

18% CP PROTEIN TURKEY LAYER MASH (20WKS-TILL CULLING)

INGREDIENTS	IN 100KG	IN 500KG	1N 1000KG
Maize	35.50	177.50	355.00
Guinea corn	17.50	87.50	175.00
Groundnut cake	24.85	124.25	248.50
Palm kernel cake	11.50	57.50	115.00
Limestone	7.00	35.00	70.00
Bone meal	3.00	15.00	30.00
Salt	0.30	1.50	3.00
Vitamin premix	0.35	1.75	3.50

17.5% CP CRUDE PROTEIN TURKEY LAYER MASH

INGREDIENTS	IN 100KG	IN 500KG	1N 1000KG
Maize	64.00	320.00	640.00
Rice offal	8.00	40.00	80.00
Fish meal	13.55	67.75	135.50
Blood meal	3.35	16.75	33.50
Limestone	7.50	37.50	75.00
Bone meal	3.00	15.00	30.00
Salt	0.30	1.50	3.00
Vitamin premix	0.30	1.50	3.00

CHAPTER TEN
Guinea Fowl Starter

20% CP PROTEIN GUINEA FOWL STARTER MASH

(0 – 8 WKS)

INGREDIENTS	IN 100KG	IN 500KG	1N 1000KG
Maize	61.50	307.50	615.00
Rice offer	7.50	37.50	75.00
Groundnut cake	22.00	110.00	220.00
Bone meal	3.00	15.00	30.00
Salt	0.30	1.50	3.00
Vitamin premix	0.35	1.75	3.50
Blood meal	5.35	26.75	53.50

21% CP PROTEIN GUINEA FOWL STARTER MASH

INGREDIENTS	IN 100KG	IN 500KG	1N 1000KG
Guinea corn	65.00	325.00	650.00
Groundnut cake	31.35	156.75	313.50
Bone meal	3.00	15.00	30.00
Salt	0.30	1.50	3.00
Vitamin premix	0.35	1.75	3.50

21.5% CP PROTEIN GUINEA FOWL STARTER MASH

(0 – 8 WEEKS)

INGREDIENTS	IN 100KG	IN 500KG	1N 1000KG
Maize	54.00	270.00	540.00
Wheat bran	12.00	60.00	120.00
Soya bean	25.10	125.50	251.00
Blood meal	5.00	25.00	50.00
Bone meal	3.00	15.00	30.00
Lysine	0.15	0.75	1.50
Methionine	0.10	0.50	1.00
Salt	0.30	1.50	3.00
Vitamin premix	0.35	1.75	3.50

CHAPTER ELEVEN
Guinea Fowl Grower Mash

16% CP PROTEIN GUINEA FOWL GROWER MASH

(9 – 20 WEEKS)

INGREDIENTS	IN 100KG	IN 500KG	1N 1000KG
Maize	65.00	325.00	650.00
Wheat bran	16.00	80.00	160.00
Soya bean	12.90	64.50	129.00
Blood meal	2.50	12.50	25.00
Bone meal	3.00	15.00	30.00
Salt	0.30	1.50	3.00
Vitamin premix	0.30	1.50	3.00

17% CP PROTEIN GUINEA FOWL GROWER MASH

INGREDIENTS	IN 100KG	IN 500KG	1N 1000KG
Guinea corn	69.00	345.00	690.00
Rice bran	11.00	55.00	110.00
Ground cake	13.10	65.50	131.00
Blood meal	3.00	15.00	30.00
Bone meal	3.00	15.00	30.00
lysine	0.15	0.75	1.50
methionine	0.10	0.50	1.00
Salt	0.30	1.50	3.00
Vitaminpremix	0.35	1.75	3.50

CHAPTER TWELVE
Guinea Fowl Layer Mash

16% CP PROTEIN GUINEA FOWL LAYER MASH

(20wks –TILL CULLING)

INGREDIENTS	IN 100KG	IN 500KG	1N 1000KG
Maize	51.00	255.00	510.00
Rice offal	17.00	85.00	170.00
groundnut cake	16.35	81.75	163.50
Blood meal	4.00	20.00	40.00
Bone meal	3.50	17.50	35.00
Limestone	7.50	37.50	75.00
Salt	0.30	1.50	3.00
Vitamin premix	0.35	1.75	3.50

17% CP PROTEIN GUINEA FOWL LAYER MASH

INGREDIENTS	IN 100KG	IN 500KG	1N 1000KG
Guinea corn	52.00	260.00	520.00
Wheat bran	18.00	90.00	180.00
Fish meal	9.85	49.25	98.50
Palm kernel meal	6.00	30.00	60.00
Blood meal	3.00	15.00	30.00
Bone meal	3.00	15.00	30.00
Limestone	7.50	37.50	75.00
Salt	0.35	1.75	3.50
Vitamin premix	0.30	1.50	3.00

CHAPTER THIRTEEN
Duckling Starter Mash

19% CP PROTEIN DUCKLING STARTER MASH

(0 – 8 WEEKS)

INGREDIENTS	IN 100KG	IN 500KG	1N 1000KG
Maize	52.00	260.00	520.00
Rice offal	17.70	88.50	177.00
Groundnut cake	16.70	83.50	167.00
Palm kernel cake	3.00	15.00	30.00
Blood meal	7.00	35.00	70.00
Bone meal	3.00	15.00	30.00
Salt	0.30	1.50	3.00
Vitamin premix	0.30	1.50	3.00

19.5% CP PROTEIN DUCKLING STARTER MASH

INGREDIENTS	IN 100KG	IN 500KG	1N 1000KG
Guinea corn	46.50	232.50	465.00
Beniseed	7.00	35.00	70.00
Wheat bran	16.35	81.75	163.50
Fish meal	9.00	45.00	90.00
Cotton seed meal	17.00	85.00	170.00
Limestone	3.50	17.50	35.00
Salt	0.35	1.75	3.50
Vitamin premix	0.30	1.50	3.00

CHAPTER FOURTEEN

Duck Grower Mash

17.5% CP PROTEIN DUCK GROWER MASH

(9 – 20 WEEKS)

INGREDIENTS	IN 100KG	IN 500KG	1N 1000KG
Millet	26.50	132.50	265.00
Maize	40.20	201.00	402.00
Rice bran	13.00	65.00	130.00
Soya bean meal	13.65	68.25	136.50
Blood meal	3.00	15.00	30.00
Bone meal	3.00	15.00	30.00
Salt	0.30	1.50	3.00
Vitamin premix	0.35	1.75	3.50

15.5% CP PROTEIN DUCK GROWER MASH

INGREDIENTS	IN 100KG	IN 500KG	1N 1000KG
Guinea corn	65.75	328.75	657.50
Maize bran	21.60	108.00	216.00
Fish meal	9.00	45.00	90.00
Salt	0.30	1.50	3.00
Bone meal	3.00	15.00	30.00
Vitamin premix	0.35	1.75	3.50

CHAPTER FIFTEEN
Duck Layer Mash

17% CP PROTEIN DUCK LAYER MASH
(20wks till culling)

INGREDIENTS	IN 100KG	IN 500KG	1N 1000KG
Maize	58.00	290.00	580.00
Rice offal	9.50	47.50	95.00
Groundnut cake	17.60	88.00	176.00
Blood meal	4.30	21.50	43.00
Bone meal	3.00	15.00	30.00
Limestone	7.00	35.00	70.00
Salt	0.30	1.50	3.00
Vitamin premix	0.30	1.50	3.00

18% CP PROTEIN DUCK LAYER MASH

INGREDIENTS	IN 100KG	IN 500KG	1N 1000KG
Guinea corn	61.00	305.00	610.00
Wheat bran	10.20	51.00	102.00
Fish meal	5.50	27.50	55.00
Soya bean meal	9.70	48.50	97.00
Blood meal	2.50	12.50	25.00
Bone meal	3.00	15.00	30.00
Limestone	7.50	37.50	75.00
Vitamin premix	0.30	1.50	3.00
Salt	0.30	1.50	3.00

CHAPTER SIXTEEN

Quail Starter Feed

20% CP PROTEIN QUAIL STARTER MASH

(0 – 3 WEEKS)

INGREDIENTS	IN 100KG	IN 500KG	1N 1000KG
Maize	61.50	307.50	615.00
Rice offer	7.50	37.50	75.00
Groundnut cake	22.00	110.00	220.00
Bone meal	3.00	15.00	30.00
Salt	0.30	1.50	3.00
Vitamin premix	0.35	1.75	3.50
Blood meal	5.35	26.75	53.50

21% CP PROTEIN QUAIL STARTER MASH

INGREDIENTS	IN 100KG	IN 500KG	1N 1000KG
Guinea corn	65.00	325.00	650.00
Groundnut cake	31.35	156.75	313.50
Bone meal	3.00	15.00	30.00
Salt	0.30	1.50	3.00
Vitamin premix	0.35	1.75	3.50

21.5% CP PROTEIN QUAIL STARTER MASH

(0 – 3 WEEKS)

INGREDIENTS	IN 100KG	IN 500KG	1N 1000KG
Maize	54.00	270.00	540.00
Wheat bran	12.00	60.00	120.00
Soya bean	25.10	125.50	251.00
Blood meal	5.00	25.00	50.00
Bone meal	3.00	15.00	30.00
Lysine	0.15	0.75	1.50
Methionine	0.10	0.50	1.00
Salt	0.30	1.50	3.00
Vitamin premix	0.35	1.75	3.50

CHAPTER SEVENTEEN
Quail Grower Mash

16% CP PROTEIN QUAIL GROWER MASH (4–7 WEEKS)

INGREDIENTS	IN 100KG	IN 500KG	1N 1000KG
Maize	65.00	325.00	650.00
Wheat bran	16.00	80.00	160.00
Soya bean	12.90	64.50	129.00
Blood meal	2.50	12.50	25.00
Bone meal	3.00	15.00	30.00
Salt	0.30	1.50	3.00
Vitamin premix	0.30	1.50	3.00

17% CP PROTEIN QUAIL GROWER MASH

INGREDIENTS	IN 100KG	IN 500KG	1N 1000KG
Maize	69.00	345.00	690.00
Wheat offal	11.00	55.00	110.00
Ground cake	13.10	65.50	131.00
Blood meal	3.00	15.00	30.00
Bone meal	3.00	15.00	30.00
lysine	0.15	0.75	1.50
methionine	0.10	0.50	1.00
Salt	0.30	1.50	3.00
Vitamin premix	0.35	1.75	3.50

CHAPTER EIGHTEEN

Quail Layer Mash

16% CP PROTEIN QUAIL LAYER MASH

(8wks –TILL CULLING)

INGREDIENTS	IN 100KG	IN 500KG	1N 1000KG
Maize	51.00	255.00	510.00
Wheat offal	17.00	85.00	170.00
groundnut cake	16.35	81.75	163.50
Blood meal	4.00	20.00	40.00
Bone meal	3.50	17.50	35.00
Limestone	7.50	37.50	75.00
Salt	0.30	1.50	3.00
Vitamin premix	0.35	1.75	3.50

17% CP PROTEIN QUAIL LAYER MASH

INGREDIENTS	IN 100KG	IN 500KG	1N 1000KG
Guinea corn	52.00	260.00	520.00
Rice offal	18.00	90.00	180.00
Fish meal	9.85	49.25	98.50
Palm kernel meal	6.00	30.00	60.00
Blood meal	3.00	15.00	30.00
Bone meal	3.00	15.00	30.00
Limestone	7.50	37.50	75.00
Salt	0.35	1.75	3.50
Vitamin premix	0.30	1.50	3.00

Example

INGREDIENTS	IN 100KG	IN 500KG	1N 1000KG
Maize	61.50	307.50	615.00
Rice offer	7.50	37.50	75.00
Groundnut cake	22.00	110.00	220.00
Bone meal	3.00	15.00	30.00
Salt	0.30	1.50	3.00
Vitamin premix	0.35	1.75	3.50
Blood meal	5.35	26.75	53.50

To calculate 50kg you have to divide each ingredient in 100kg by 2

Maize   **61.50/2 = 30.75**

Rice offer   **7.50/2 = 3.75**

Groundnut cake   **22.00/2 = 11.00**

Bone meal   **3.00/2 = 1.50**

Salt   **0.30/2 = 0.15**

Vitamin premix   **0.35/2 = 0.17**

Blood meal   **5.35/2 = 2.68**

TOTAL = 50KG

Example:

50kg divide each ingredients by 2 just like the example above to get 25kg of feed formula

Example:

Maize   **30.75**

Rice offer   **3.75**

Groundnut cake   **11.00**

Bone meal   **1.50**

Salt   **0.15**

Vitamin premix   **0.17**

Blood meal   **2.68**

TOTAL = 50KG

See Example below:

To calculate 25kg, you divide each ingredient in 50kg by 2

Example:

Maize   **30.75/2 = 15.375**

Rice offer   **3.75/2 = 1.875**

Groundnut cake **11.00/2 = 5.5**

Bone meal   **1.50/2 = 0.75**

Salt   **0.15/2 = 0.075**

Vitamin premix   **0.17/2 = 0.085**

Blood meal   **2.68/2 = 1.34**

                            TOTAL = 25KG

To calculate 5kg, you divide each ingredient in 25kg by 5

Example:

Maize   **15.375/5**

Rice offer   **1.875/5**

Groundnut cake   **5.5/5**

Bone meal   **0.75/5**

Salt   **0.075/5**

Vitamin premix   **0.085/5**

Blood meal   **1.34/5**

TOTAL = 25KG

To calculate 200kg, you multiply each ingredient in 100kg by 2

Example:

Maize   61.50 x 2 = 123

Rice offer   7.50 x 2 = 15

Groundnut cake   22.00 x 2 = 44

Bone meal   3.00 x 2 = 6

Salt   0.30 x 2 = 0.6

Vitamin premix   0.35 x 2 = 0.7

Blood meal   5.35 x 2 = 10.7

                 TOTAL = 200KG

To calculate 300kg, you multiply each ingredient in 100kg by 3

Example:

Maize   **61.50 x 3 = 184.5**

Rice offer   **7.50 x 3 = 22.5**

Groundnut cake   **22.00 x 3 = 66**

Bone meal   **3.00 x 3 = 9**

Salt   **0.30 x 3 = 0.9**

Vitamin premix   **0.35 x 3 = 1.05**

Blood meal   **5.35 x 3 = 16.05**

TOTAL = 300KG

To calculate 400kg, you multiply each ingredient in 100kg by 4

Example:

Maize   **61.50 x 4 = 246**

Rice offer   **7.50 x 4 = 30**

Groundnut cake   **22.00 x 4 = 88**

Bone meal   **3.00 x 4 = 12**

Salt   **0.30 x 4 = 1.2**

Vitamin premix   **0.35 x 4 = 1.4**

Blood meal   **5.35 x 4 = 21.4**

TOTAL = 400G

To calculate 600kg, you multiply each ingredient in 100kg by 6

Example:

Maize   **61.50 x 6 = 369**

Rice offer   **7.50 x 6 = 45**

Groundnut cake **22.00 x 6 = 132**

Bone meal   **3.00 x 6 = 18**

Salt   **0.30 x 6 = 1.8**

Vitamin premix   **0.35 x 6 = 2.1**

Blood meal   **5.35 x 6 = 32.1**

TOTAL = 600KG

To calculate 700kg, you multiply each ingredient in 100kg by 7

Example:

Maize   **61.50 x 7 = 430.5**

Rice offer   **7.50 x 7 = 52.5**

Groundnut cake   **22.00 x 7 = 154**

Bone meal   **3.00 x 7 = 21**

Salt   **0.30 x 7 = 2.1**

Vitamin premix   **0.35 x 7 = 2.45**

Blood meal   **5.35 x 7 = 37.45**

TOTAL = 700KG

To calculate 800kg, you multiply each ingredient in 100kg by 8

Example:

Maize   **61.50 x 8 = 492**

Rice offer   **7.50 x 8 = 60**

Groundnut cake   **22.00 x 8 = 176**

Bone meal   **3.00 x 8 = 24**

Salt   **0.30 x 8 = 2.4**

Vitamin premix   **0.35 x 8 = 2.8**

Blood meal   **5.35 x 8 = 42.8**

TOTAL = 800KG

To calculate 1000kg, you multiply each ingredient in 500kg by 2

To calculate 2000kg, you multiply each ingredient in 1000kg by 2

To calculate 5000kg, you multiply each ingredient in 1000kg by 5

Note: The examples above shows how you can easily calculate any feed ingredients to get the appropriate feed formula